WHAT JESUS SAYS
ABOUT EARTH'S
FINAL DAYS

WHAT JESUS SAYS ABOUT EARTH'S FINAL DAYS

MARK HITCHCOCK

Multnomah® Publishers *Sisters, Oregon*

What Jesus Says About Earth's Final Days
published by Multnomah Publishers, Inc.

© 2003 by Mark Hitchcock
International Standard Book Number: 1-59052-208-7

Cover design by Kirk DouPonce-UDG/DesignWorks
Cover images by Corbis and Photodisc

Multnomah is a trademark of Multnomah Publishers, Inc.,
and is registered in the U.S. Patent and Trademark Office.
The colophon is a trademark of Multnomah Publishers, Inc.

Printed in the United States of America

For information:
MULTNOMAH PUBLISHERS, INC. • P.O. BOX 1720 • SISTERS, OR 97759

Library of Congress Cataloging-in-Publication Data

Hitchcock, Mark.
    What Jesus says about earth's final days / by Mark Hitchcock.
        p. cm.
Includes bibliographical references.
    ISBN 1-59052-208-7 (pbk.)
    1. Second Advent—Biblical teaching.
    2. Bible. N.T.—Criticism, interpretation, etc.   I. Title.
    BT886.3.H58 2003
    236'.9—dc21

                         2003010157

03 04 05 06 07 08—9 8 7 6 5 4 3 2 1 0

To Dr. David Cotten,
my pastor, teacher, and friend.
Words cannot adequately express what your
consistent example of living and teaching the
Word have meant and continue to mean to me
and my entire family.

"When the Chief Shepherd appears,
you will receive the unfading crown of glory."
1 PETER 5:4

CONTENTS

INTRODUCTION

Gulf War II
Weapons of Mass Destruction
North Korea and the Axis of Evil
AIDS Epidemic
SARS
Terrorist Threats

Does it sometimes seem like the world is spinning out of control? Do you find youself feeling anxious and worried, and even a bit depressed, about where our world is headed?

If so, this book is for you. In times like these it's critical for us to pay attention to the words of Jesus Christ, because He's the only person who ever lived or ever will live who knows the future. And He is so gracious that He's given us His personal forecast for the future of planet earth.

Jesus knows the future. Nothing takes Him by surprise. He's not worried one bit about what's ahead. He not only knows what's coming; He's in total control.

So take a deep breath and rest in Him. He has a plan that He's working out for His own glory. The purpose of this book is to unfold that plan so that we can know what's ahead and can live more faithfully for Him until He comes. Won't you join me as we listen to the Master's voice concerning earth's final days

His words will comfort you.

His words will challenge you.

His words will call you to live each day in light of His coming.

As with all the other books in the End Times Answers series, I will assume that the reader has at least a basic grasp of the main events of the end times. However, to help make sure that we're all on the same page, here's a brief overview of some of the key terms you will see sprinkled throughout this book.

The Rapture of the Church to Heaven

The Rapture is an event that could occur at any moment. It's a signless event. At the Rapture, all who have personally trusted in Jesus Christ as their Savior, the living and the dead, will be caught up to meet the Lord in the air and will go with Him back up to heaven. Then they will return again with Him, back to earth, at least seven years later at His second coming (John 14:1–3; 1 Corinthians 15:50–58; 1 Thessalonians 4:13–18).

THE SEVEN-YEAR TRIBULATION PERIOD

The Tribulation is the final seven years of this age. It will begin with a peace treaty between Israel and the Antichrist and will end with the second coming of Christ back to earth. During this time the Lord will pour out His wrath upon the earth in successive waves of judgment. But the Lord will also pour out His grace by saving millions of people during this time (Revelation 6–19).

THE THREE-AND-A-HALF-YEAR WORLD EMPIRE OF THE ANTICHRIST

During the last half of the Tribulation, the Antichrist will rule the world politically, economically, and religiously. The entire world will give allegiance to him or suffer persecution and death (Revelation 13:1–18).

THE CAMPAIGN OF ARMAGEDDON

The campaign or War of Armageddon is the final event of the Great Tribulation. It will occur when all the armies of the earth gather together to come against Israel and attempt once and for all to eradicate the Jewish people (Revelation 14:19–20; 16:12–16; 19:19–21).

THE SECOND COMING OF CHRIST TO EARTH

The climactic event of human history is the literal, physical, visible, glorious return of Jesus Christ to planet earth. He will destroy the armies of the world gathered in Israel and set up his kingdom on earth, which will last for one thousand years (Revelation 19:11–21).

God's Blueprint for the End Times

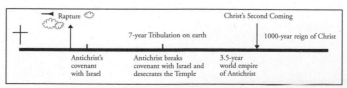

11

May the Lord use this book to help us hear what Jesus says about earth's final days. May we all obey His command to be alert, busy, and ready when He comes.

"Be like men who are waiting for their Master when He returns" (Luke 12:36).

Maranatha!

"Our Lord, come!"

Mark Hitchcock

CHAPTER ONE

JESUS AND THE FUTURE

"Heaven and earth will pass away,
but My words will not pass away."
MATTHEW 24:35

There's a poignant old saying, "The future's not what it used to be."

When we look around today, we may be tempted, now more than ever, to agree with this analysis of the world situation. The world today is a more dangerous place than it's ever been. Uncertainty abounds. We see and hear things on television that we never thought we would live to see. The future often troubles us.

But not Jesus. The future is no problem for Him.

He talked about the future with confidence, assurance, and hope. And not just in some nebulous, general, vague fashion. Jesus gave meticulous, detailed, specific prophecies concerning events in the distant future. Events that are still future in *our* day. Yet Jesus gazed into that distant future with piercing perception and spoke of events that were then more than two thousand years away.

But before we jump into the details, let's get a little more background from the four Gospels on Jesus' relationship to the future.[1]

THREE TRUTHS ABOUT JESUS AND THE FUTURE

TRUTH #1: Jesus talked a great deal about the future.

It's common nowadays to hear people say something like, "I don't worry about the end times or Bible prophecy—I just live each day for Jesus and leave all that up to Him. No one knows what's going to happen anyway."

Maybe you've said something like that yourself—perhaps even recently.

But nothing could be further from the biblical

truth. Jesus wants His followers to know what's coming. That's why He spent such a great deal of time talking about the future. In fact, He may have talked about the future more than any person who ever lived. Jesus wasn't preoccupied with it in an unbalanced way, but He *did* emphasize its importance on many occasions.

Here's a brief list of some of Jesus' more familiar teachings concerning the future.

THE SCRIPTURE	THE SUBJECT
Matthew 13:24–30, 36–43, 47–50	Final Judgment
Matthew 20:1–16	Rewards
Matthew 8:11–12; 22:1–4	Christ's Kingdom
Matthew 24–25 (see also Mark 13 and Luke 21)	Signs of His Coming
Luke 12:35–38	Staying Ready for His Coming
Luke 16:19–31	The Afterlife
Luke 17:22–37	Conditions on Earth at His Coming
Luke 19:11–17	Accountability and Rewards

It's crystal clear from His many discussions, debates, and discourses that Jesus wants His followers to know what's coming. In Matthew 24:25, Jesus said, "Behold, I have told you in advance." Again in Mark 13:23, He said, "But take heed; behold, I have told you everything in advance."

Don't ever let anyone tell you that Jesus didn't bother with the future.

TRUTH #2: Jesus sharply criticized people for not knowing about the future.

In Matthew 16:1–3, Jesus rebuked the self-righteous Pharisees for their blindness to the signs of the times. Jesus was performing signs all around them that fulfilled Old Testament prophecies and proved that He was the long-awaited Messiah.

The Pharisees and Sadducees came up, and testing [Jesus], they asked Him to show them a sign from heaven. But He answered and said to them, "When it is evening, you say, 'It will be fair weather, for the sky is red.' And in the morning, 'There will be a storm today, for the sky is red and threatening.' Do you know how to discern the appearance of the sky, but cannot discern the signs of the times?" (Matthew 16:1–3)

At Jesus' first coming, the nation of Israel as a whole was blind to the many signs all around them that Messiah had come. The Old Testament had clearly prophesied many things concerning Messiah's person and works. Yet, the people didn't put it all together. Why? Because many of them were ignorant of the prophetic word, or just didn't take the time and effort to really understand what it was saying.

People back then aren't a whole lot different from most people today. They wouldn't think of missing the evening weather on the news, but they totally neglect the Word and what it says about the signs of the times. The people in Jesus' day missed the clear signs of His first coming. Likewise, many today are oblivious of the signs of His second coming.

What's clear is that Jesus expects us to discern the signs of the times *whenever* we live, and understand what time it is in terms of what matters most.

Let us consider how to stimulate one another to love and good deeds, not forsaking our own assembling together, as is the habit of some, but encouraging one another; and all the more, as you see the day drawing near. (Hebrews 10:24–25)

Obviously, we have to be looking for Christ's coming to carry out this exhortation. After all, how in the world can we ever hope to "see the day drawing near" if we aren't even looking for it, or have no idea what we are looking for?[2]

Of course, we should never engage in wild speculation or set dates for Christ's coming. But we should do the best we can to understand the signs of the times. To determine as best we can the season—the day and hour—in which we live. Jesus calls us to investigate His prophecies and to know our times.

TRUTH #3: Jesus always talked about the future to change the way we live in the present.

Jesus was no pie-in-the-sky prophet. He always related future events to the present. We must never forget this important truth. Jesus' teaching on the future always placed present demands upon His hearers. If we study Jesus' teaching about earth's final days just to have our imaginations tantalized, to fill our minds with time charts, or to satisfy our curiosity, we have completely missed His intent.

Jesus' pronouncements about the future always carry specific application for the here and now.

THREE REASONS WHY WE CAN TRUST JESUS' FORECAST OF THE FUTURE

Clearly, Jesus talked a lot about the future. About His second coming. About man's eternal destiny. About earth's final days. But there have been many prophets professing to know the future.

Nostradamus

Edward Cayce (known as the "Sleeping Prophet")

Jeane Dixon (the self-proclaimed modern prophetess)

Why should we listen to Jesus? What makes His voice rise above all the rest? There are three key things that make Jesus utterly unique.

REASON #1: His Person

Very simply, Jesus is God. Yes, He's also fully man. But He is God.

As God and man in one person, Jesus has one foot

in eternity, one foot in time and space. He knows the beginning from the end. But He also walked on this earth and revealed to us what is coming for this planet.

If you are ever tempted to doubt whether Jesus knows the future, just stop and think about how Jesus is described in the book of Revelation.

The Names and Titles of Christ in Revelation
1. Jesus Christ (1:1)
2. Faithful Witness (1:5)
3. Firstborn of the Dead (1:5)
4. Ruler of the Kings of the Earth (1:5)
5. Alpha and Omega (1:8)
6. The One Who Is and Who Was and Who Is to Come (1:8)
7. The Almighty (1:8)
8. Son of Man (1:13)
9. The First and the Last (1:17; 2:8)
10. The Living One (2:8)
11. The One Who Holds the Seven Stars in His Right Hand (2:1)
12. The One Who Walks Among the Seven Golden Lampstands (2:1)
13. The One Who Has the Sharp Two-Edged Sword (2:12)

14. The Son of God (2:18)
15. The One Who Has Eyes like a Flame of Fire (2:18)
16. The One Whose Feet Are like Burnished Bronze (2:18)
17. The One Who Has the Seven Spirits of God and the Seven Stars (3:1)
18. He Who Is Holy, Who Is True (3:7)
19. The One Who Has the Key of David (3:7)
20. The Amen (3:14)
21. The Faithful and True Witness (3:14)
22. The Beginning of the Creation of God (3:14)
23. The Lion from the Tribe of Judah (5:5)
24. The Root of David (5:5)
25. The Lamb (5:6)
26. O Lord, Holy and True (6:10)
27. Their Lord (11:8)
28. A Son, a Male Child, Who Is to Rule All the Nations with a Rod of Iron(12:5)
29. Her Child (12:5)
30. O Lord God, the Almighty (15:3)
31. King of the Nations (15:3)
32. Faithful and True (19:11)
33. The Word of God (19:13)

34. King of Kings, and Lord of Lords (19:16)
35. The Bright Morning Star (22:16)

The Bible also makes it absolutely clear that only God knows the future.

Thus says the LORD, the King of Israel and his Redeemer, the LORD of hosts: "I am the first and I am the last, and there is no God besides Me. Who is like Me? Let him proclaim and declare it; yes, let him recount it to Me in order, from the time that I established the ancient nation. And let them declare to them the things that are coming and the events that are going to take place. Do not tremble and do not be afraid; have I not long since announced it to you and declared it? And you are My witnesses. Is there any God besides Me, or is there any other Rock? I know of none." (Isaiah 44:6–8)

"Remember this, and be assured; recall it to mind, you transgressors. Remember the former things long past, for I am God, and there is no other; I am God, and there is no one like

Me, declaring the end from the beginning, and from ancient times things which have not been done, saying, 'My purpose will be established, and I will accomplish all My good pleasure.'" (Isaiah 46:8–10)

In addition, since Jesus is God we know that He cannot lie. There is absolutely no falsehood in Him.

God is not a man, that He should lie, nor a son of man, that He should repent; has He said, and will He not do it? Or has He spoken, and will He not make it good? (Numbers 23:19)

In the hope of eternal life, which God, who cannot lie, promised long ages ago. (Titus 1:2)

Jesus knows the future, and everything He says about it is totally trustworthy!

REASON #2: His Prophecies

During His earthly ministry, Jesus was recognized over and over again as a prophet (Matthew 21:11; Mark 6:15; Luke 7:16; John 4:19). Jesus knew things and said things that astonished His listeners. But how can we be sure that His prophecies concerning the future will come true?

The only surefire way is to look at His track record. Consider just a few of the prophecies that Jesus gave while He was on earth that have already been fulfilled:

1. Jesus predicted the manner of His death (Matthew 20:19; 26:2).
2. Jesus predicted the exact day of His death (Matthew 26:2).
3. Jesus predicted Judas's betrayal (Matthew 26:20–25).
4. Jesus predicted Peter's denial (Matthew 26:33–34).
5. Jesus predicted the apostles' desertion of Him (Matthew 26:31).
6. Jesus predicted His resurrection (Matthew 12:40; 16:21; 17:9).
7. Jesus predicted the exact day of His resurrection (Matthew 12:40; 16:21; 20:19).
8. Jesus predicted the destruction of Jerusalem (Matthew 24:1–2).

Jesus was 100 percent accurate, 100 percent of the time! Quite a record. He was the prophet *par excellence* that Moses said would one day come (Deuteronomy 18:15).

Reason #3: His Passion

We should listen to Jesus not only because of who He is and what He said, but because of what He did for us.

> But God demonstrates His own love toward us, in that while we were yet sinners, Christ died for us. (Romans 5:8)

Jesus is not only the Alpha and the Omega, the Beginning and the End, the First and the Last, the Lion of the tribe of Judah, and the Word of God, but He is also the pure, spotless Lamb of God who willingly laid down His life and purchased our pardon.

Do you know what the number one title for Jesus is, in the book of Revelation?

The lamb!

Jesus is referred to as the lamb twenty-eight times in the last book of the Bible. Amid all the conquest, victory, judgment, and majesty in the book of Revelation, God never wants us to lose sight of His lamb, the Lord Jesus Christ. Everything in Revelation is made possible because of the Lamb of God who takes away the sin of the world (John 1:29).

Surely we can trust the word of the One who became sin *for* us, who laid down His life for His sheep. He would never lead us astray.

So again—why should you and I listen to Jesus and what He says about earth's final days?

Because He's God in human flesh. He knows what's coming. He lives in the future. And because every one of His prophecies that's come to pass so far was fulfilled exactly as He said it would be, *just as the remainder will be fulfilled!*

But most of all, because He died and rose again for us and would never lead us astray.

"He Who Has Ears to Hear!"

One of my favorite lines from the lips of Jesus is His oft-repeated statement, "He who has ears to hear, let him hear." Jesus is saying, "Look, if you have a set of ears on your head you'd better use them and listen up to what I'm about to say." It's a direct challenge to us to be spiritually sensitive to the words of Jesus. The responsibility to listen carefully to Him is serious.

As we move into a careful study of Jesus' forecast

for the future, I can't think of a better reminder. Let's listen carefully and willingly to the mighty Master as He leads us down the corridors of time to the end of the age. And be ready to follow His instructions about how to live while we wait for that day to come.

JESUS' BLUEPRINT OF THE END

O ther than the book of Revelation, the longest, most important passage in the New Testament on end-time prophecy is Matthew 24–25. It's often referred to as the Olivet Discourse because these chapters are the record of a great sermon Jesus preached from the Mount of Olives.

Sometimes this final sermon of Jesus is called the "mini apocalypse" because it's almost like the *Reader's Digest* condensed version of the apocalypse, or book of Revelation. In this sermon, Jesus distilled the end times down to their most basic elements.

In His great prophetic sermon in Matthew 24–25, Jesus gave the basic outline of the events that will immediately precede His coming. It's Jesus' forecast of the future. And there is no place in the Bible that gives a clearer, more concise overview of what's going to happen during earth's final days.

THE SETTING OF THE SERMON

The setting was Jesus' farewell message to His confused band of disciples. Jesus had been with them for more than three years, and they still did not understand what was about to happen to their leader. Two days later, on Friday, He would be nailed to a Roman cross and would suffer a cruel, barbaric death. But it was still Wednesday of the final week of His life, and from a hill east of Jerusalem, called the Mount of Olives, Jesus unveiled a sweeping panorama of the future for His disciples.

Jesus and the Twelve slowly ascended the summit of the hill that overlooked the temple mount in Jerusalem, two hundred feet below. It was Passover season so the temple precinct would have been teeming with pilgrims. When they reached the summit, Jesus seated Himself on a rock, and four of the disciples, Peter, James, John, and Andrew, approached Him privately and asked a penetrating question that had probably been burning in their hearts for some time.

"Tell us, when will these things happen, and what

will be the sign of Your coming, and of the end of the age?" (Matthew 24:3).

The question they asked is one that many are asking today, "When will the world come to an end?" As the late afternoon shadows lengthened over the city of Jerusalem, Israel's premiere prophet began to paint a riveting portrait of the end of the age.[3]

THE SUBJECT OF THE SERMON

Some of the most important questions about this sermon are: What time period does it cover? What events is it describing? Is it talking about something that has already occurred? Or is it portraying earth's final days?

This is much more than just an academic, philosophical issue because the answer to this question determines what you believe Jesus actually said about the future.

There are three main views concerning the time period presented in the Olivet Discourse. Understanding a little bit about each of these views will help us put Jesus' words in proper perspective and serve as the bedrock for the rest of this book.[4]

Let's look briefly at each of these views.

VIEW #1: All the events in Matthew 24 are past (The Preterist View)

The word "preterism" comes from the Latin word *preter,* which means "past."

Therefore, proponents of this view contend that all the events in Matthew 24:4–31 were fulfilled in A.D. 70 when Jerusalem was destroyed by the Romans. They maintain that Jesus actually did "come again" in judgment in a "cloud coming" in A.D. 70, to destroy Jerusalem.

While there are many aspects to this view, there are two principal issues that bring preterists to this conclusion.

First, they believe that Jesus is answering the question of the disciples, "When will these things be?" That is, when will Jerusalem be destroyed as Jesus had just predicted? (Matthew 24:1–3). For preterists, this sets the stage for the entire chapter.

The problem here is that preterists focus on "When will these things be?" But they ignore the other parts of the question, "And what will be the sign of Your coming, and of the end of the age?" While it is possible that the disciples had two or three separate questions in mind, more likely they were thinking of one big question with three parts. Clearly, their question focuses on the return of Christ and the end of the world. For the disciples, who thought in terms of the Old Testament prophecies, the destruction of the temple, the coming of the Messiah, and the end of the world all comprised one great complex, or matrix, of events (Zechariah 14:1–11). They couldn't envision a destruction of the temple apart from the end of the age. For them it was all part of one big climax.

So, Jesus basically ignores the first part of their question and tells them about the sign of His coming and the end of the age, knowing that that's what they really wanted to know about.

Second, preterists put great stock in Matthew 24:34: "Truly I say to you, this generation will not pass away until all these things take place."

They argue that "this generation" must refer to the generation that originally heard the words of Jesus. In other words, the generation that heard Jesus' sermon must be the generation that sees the fulfillment of all Jesus said. And the only event in that generation that could even come close to fulfilling these words was the destruction of Jerusalem in A.D. 70.

However, in the context, "this generation" probably refers to those living during the Tribulation who will personally witness the events described in Matthew 24:4–31. Jesus is emphasizing that the same generation that sees the specific signs of the times, and experiences the Great Tribulation, will also witness the Second Coming.[5] Those who are alive to see the beginning of the birth pangs will also witness the birth.

To me, there are two insurmountable obstacles for the preterist view to overcome. First, they say that Matthew 24:4–31 was fulfilled in the destruction of Jerusalem. Yet, in Matthew 24, Jesus never actually describes the destruction of the city or even the temple itself. Rather, the focus is on the deliverance of the Jewish remnant.

Second, one has to stretch the limits of credulity to fit the signs and events recorded in Matthew 24 into the events of A.D. 70. Just a simple reading of Matthew 24:29–31 and the cosmic signs that it mentions reveals that nothing even close to this transpired in A.D. 70 in Jerusalem.[6]

> ## THE PRETERIST VIEW OF THE OLIVET DISCOURSE
>
> The destruction of Jerusalem in A.D. 70 was Christ's "cloud coming" to earth described in verses 4–31.

VIEW #2: Some of the events in Matthew 24 are being fulfilled in the present age, while some are future (The Entire Age View)

Others hold that Matthew 24:4–14 describes conditions that will exist between Christ's ascension back to heaven in A.D. 33 and the final onset of the Tribulation. In other words, Matthew 24:4–14 lists general signs, events, and situations that mark the progress of the present age. As these signs intensify in the present age, they serve as signs that the end of the age is approaching.[7]

Those who hold this view believe that Matthew 24:15–28 describes the events of the future Tribulation period. So, Jesus was giving an overview of the course of the entire age between His two comings.

It is true that many of the conditions in Matthew 24:4–14 have been present throughout the entire church age, but the general nature of these events cannot be signs of Christ's coming. It is much more consistent to view all the events in Matthew 24:4–28 as future.

Jesus said, "So, you too, when you see *all these things*, recognize that He is near, right at the door" (Matthew 24:33, emphasis added). It seems clear to me that all the signs in Matthew 24:4–28 are a package deal. Like birth pangs, once they start they will be fulfilled in a very short period of time.

Jesus also likened *all* the signs in Matthew 24:4–28 to the budding of a fig tree (Matthew 24:32–33). When the fig tree begins to bud, you can know for sure that summer is coming very soon.[8] You can almost count the days until it will arrive. In the same way, when the first signs of Matthew 24 begin, Christ will come very quickly—seven years later.[9] The final "week" of years, or seven years of this age, will begin when Antichrist makes a covenant with Israel.

THE ENTIRE AGE VIEW OF THE OLIVET DISCOURSE		
The Present Age	The Tribulation	The Second Coming
vv. 4–14	vv. 15–28	vv. 29–31

The signs escalate in intensity as the end times approach. Also, Jesus' descriptions of the events become progressively more specific.

VIEW #3: All the events Jesus described in Matthew 24 are future (The Futurist View)

I believe the best view is to see all the conditions and characteristics in Matthew 24:4–28 as future events that will occur in the relatively short period of time immediately preceding the return of Christ. Therefore, I see the dramatic events Jesus lists as encompassing a relatively brief period of time—the final seven years of this age. Three key points from the surrounding context lead me to this view.

First, Jesus established the time frame for this sermon in Matthew 23:39. "For I tell you this, you will never see me again until you say, 'Bless the one who comes in the name of the Lord!'" (NLT).

Jesus was telling His disciples that He was going to leave this world but that He would come again only when the Jewish people would repent and receive Him as their Messiah. This statement is very significant; it forms the backdrop and context for what Jesus says in Matthew 24. Jesus is saying that Jewish repentance is the ultimate event that will trigger His return. Obviously, this did not happen in A.D. 70. In fact, it was a lack of Jewish repentance that brought on that devastation.

However, at the end of the future Tribulation, the Jewish people will repent and their Messiah will return to rescue them from Antichrist (Zechariah 12:10).

Second, when the disciples asked Jesus about the end of the age, it only makes sense, given their grid of the Old Testament prophets, that they were thinking of the time when Messiah would come to establish His glorious kingdom in Israel. In fact, Jesus Himself had used this exact terminology, "the end of the age," on two previous occasions to refer to the time of final judgment (Matthew 13:39, 49).

Third, the scope and degree of the cataclysm described in Matthew 24:21 cannot realistically be made to fit the events of A.D. 70: "For then there will be a great tribulation, such as has not occurred since the beginning of the world until now, nor ever will."

I agree wholeheartedly with this concise summary by John MacArthur.

It seems more sensible and more consistent, therefore, to take a futurist approach with respect to the Olivet Discourse—to interpret the entire discourse as a prophetic picture of a "generation" and events that would take place long after the destruction of Jerusalem in A.D. 70. These are events that will immediately precede Christ's coming to establish His kingdom, and therefore they are events that are yet future even today.[10]

Therefore, I believe that the purpose of this sermon by Jesus was to outline for Israel the events that would immediately lead up to the return of their Messiah to establish His kingdom on earth and to call them to faithfulness in view of that coming.

FUTURIST VIEW OF THE OLIVET DISCOURSE	
The Seven-Year Tribulation	The Second Coming
vv. 4–28	vv. 29–31

THE SEQUENCE OF EVENTS IN THE SERMON

Before we dive into the details of Jesus' word to us concerning earth's final days, there's one more bit of housekeeping that will help guide us along.

Jesus follows an orderly chronological sequence in unfolding the major events of earth's final days. He employs four key phrases that move the listener or reader along to the climax. We will examine each of these four phrases, one at a time, in the next four chapters. But here's just a brief introduction to each of them so that when they pop up later you will already be familiar with them.

"the beginning of birth pangs" (24:8)
This is the first three-and-a-half years of the coming seven-year Tribulation period. The beginning of these birth pangs is unfolded in Matthew 24:4–14.

"the abomination of desolation" (24:15)
This definitive event will transpire at the midpoint of the seven-year Tribulation period.

"great tribulation" (24:21)
This refers to the last three-and-a-half years of the Tribulation period. It will be the final brief period of

the age. It will be "the end of the age" that Jesus' disciples asked Him about.

"But immediately after the tribulation of those days"
(24:29)
Beginning in Matthew 24:29, the Second Coming of Christ is chronicled. Notice it will come "immediately after the Tribulation of those days."

This sequence can be more easily grasped by looking at this simple chart.

THE OLIVET DISCOURSE—BLUEPRINT OF THE END TIMES			
The Seven-Year Tribulation Period			The Second Coming
vv. 4–14	vv. 15–20	vv. 21–28	vv. 29–31
The Beginning Birth Pangs	Abomination of Desolation	The Great Tribulation	Jesus Returns
First Three-and-a-Half Years of the Tribulation	Middle of the Tribulation	Second Three-and-a-Half Years of the Tribulation	After the Tribulation

A WORD FOR TODAY

The words of Jesus concerning earth's final days are just as relevant today as when they were given, and even more timely for us today. They speak of a still-future time when Jesus will come again to planet earth, and should fill our hearts with anticipation and alertness.

According to Jesus, earth's final days get started with what He vividly described as "birth pangs." He couldn't have chosen a more appropriate picture.

Get ready for the first contraction.

CHAPTER THREE

BIRTH PANGS

My wife, Cheryl, and I have two sons. As every parent will understand, they are the joy of our life together. But their entrance into this world was anything but a joyful experience. At least for Cheryl.

Our first son was born eleven weeks prematurely, so we never attended those childbirth classes that everyone goes to. I had no clue about what was coming. But I knew there was something important about breathing. So, like a good husband I sat there next to the bed, holding my wife's hand and leading her in rhythmic breathing. I figured I could provide some moral support if nothing else.

As the labor pains intensified, my wife began to squeeze my left hand harder and harder. Before long my wedding ring was digging deep into my other fingers. My sweet little wife had a death grip on my hand.

It was all I could do not to let that become my total focus. Of course, I couldn't say anything. How could I complain about my crushed hand when my wife was laying there feeling like her insides were coming out? (That's how she described it later to me).

Finally, when I thought I couldn't hold out any longer, the doctor came in to administer the epidural.

At last! Our anguish was over.

Well, enough of the birthing room experience. But you get the point. When Jesus began to respond to the disciples' questions, Jesus employed a figure that is familiar to all of us, and very graphic—birth pains (Matthew 24:8). He was also referencing familiar Old Testament imagery that pictures the events of the end times.

> They will be terrified, pains and anguish will take hold of them; they will writhe like a woman in labor, they will look at one another in astonishment, their faces aflame. Behold, the day of the LORD is coming, cruel, with fury and burning anger, to make the land a desolation; and He will exterminate its sinners from it. (Isaiah 13:8–9)

For I heard a cry as of a woman in labor, the anguish as of one giving birth to her first child, the cry of the daughter of Zion gasping for breath, stretching out her hands, saying, "Ah, woe is me, for I faint before murderers." (Jeremiah 4:31)

For thus says the LORD, "I have heard a sound of terror, of dread, and there is no peace. Ask now, and see if a male can give birth. Why do I see every man with his hands on his loins, as a woman in childbirth? And why have all faces turned pale? Alas! for that day is great, there is none like it; and it is the time of Jacob's distress, but he will be saved from it." (Jeremiah 30:4–7)

The apostle Paul also drew upon this same analogy in 1 Thessalonians 5:3:

While they are saying, "Peace and safety!" then destruction will come upon them suddenly like labor pains upon a woman with child, and they will not escape.

We need to remember several important things about birth pangs.

First, they come without any warning. All of a sudden, out of nowhere they begin.

Second, they are irreversible. Once they begin there's no stopping them. Now, I know that today there are drugs available that can hold them off for a while. Before our first son was born, my wife was in the hospital for four weeks, taking medicine that held off the labor pains that had already begun, to give him more time to develop. But even with that strong medication, the labor pains were still irreversible. The best the physicians could do was hold them off for a while.

Third, they intensify. As the labor begins, the pangs normally aren't too severe. In fact, sometimes women aren't sure if they are even having labor pains. But a little bit of time usually removes all doubt. As the labor proceeds, the pains rapidly become stronger. Before long the pain is intense, stabbing, and unbearable.

Fourth, they get closer together. The pains not only grow harder, but they come closer and closer together. As the labor advances, the pains begin to get worse and worse, and the break between contractions becomes shorter and shorter. Finally, the blinding pain crashes and mounts relentlessly in wave after wave of crippling contractions.

With this analogy, Jesus is saying that the first events of the Tribulation will come upon the world suddenly. And, as the Tribulation period unfolds, the judgments of God will move irreversibly forward. Worst of all, the labor contractions will become more severe and closer and closer together until the world stands on the brink of total destruction. Just when the pains reach their zenith, the "birth" will take place as Jesus returns to earth as King of kings and Lord of lords.

Jesus gives a kind of checklist of nine labor pangs that will signal the beginning of the end.

THE BEGINNING OF BIRTH PANGS

PANG #1: False Messiahs

As the Tribulation begins, there will be a flood of false messiahs. After the Rapture has occurred, people all over the world will be groping for answers. And with the removal of the church, error will spread unchecked, like cancer. False messiahs will claim to know what's happening. They will have answers for the questions people are asking. In the midst of all the chaos, however, one man will rise to the forefront. He will be the ultimate, final false messiah.

The Antichrist.

He will burst on the scene as a great diplomat and peacemaker. He will enter into a covenant of peace with Israel (Daniel 9:27). This event will start the clock ticking. This is the very first birth pang!

It's interesting to me how a wave of pacifism has swept across the world in just the last decade. The universal, almost desperate cry for peace in our world today points toward this future time of peace. It may not be far away.

PANG #2: Wars and Rumors of Wars

During the first part of the Tribulation, Antichrist will solve the Middle East peace problem. He will be hailed as the world's messiah. However, in spite of his great diplomatic acumen, wars and threats of war will continue to boil over. And talk of war will fill the air.

PANG #3: Famines

The first of several natural disasters will be widespread famine. The skirmishes, wars, and ethnic conflicts will lead to the outbreak of famines all over the earth. The grim reaper won't be far behind.

> I looked, and behold, an ashen horse; and he who sat on it had the name Death; and Hades was following with him. Authority was given to them over a fourth of the earth, to kill with sword and with famine and with pestilence and by the wild beasts of the earth. (Revelation 6:8)

PANG #4: Earthquakes

As the end of the age draws near, creation will begin to groan and clear its throat in anticipation of the King's coming. Luke 21:11, a parallel passage to Matthew 24, says there will be "great earthquakes." The earthquakes will continue to increase in severity until, at the end of the Tribulation, God will shake the foundations of earth like nothing the world has ever seen!

> And there were flashes of lightning and sounds and peals of thunder; and there was a great earth-quake, such as there had not been since man came to be upon the earth, so great an earthquake

was it, and so mighty. The great city was split into three parts, and the cities of the nations fell.... And every island fled away, and the mountains were not found. (Revelation 16:18–20)

PANG #5: Plagues

According to Luke 21:11, added to all the misery of the first four birth pangs will be the outbreak of plagues, epidemics, and pestilence all over the world. All the plagues and epidemics we have seen in the past (Black Death, smallpox, influenza), and see yet today (AIDS, SARS, Ebola), are just foreshadowings of something far worse yet to come. Consider that some thirty new diseases have sprung up just since the mid-1970s, resulting in tens of millions of deaths. According to the Institute of Medicine, "Infectious diseases will continue to emerge."[11] Globalization, aided by rapid means of world travel today, has created the ideal environment for terrible plagues to run rampant over the earth in a very short time. Once they were localized, but no more. One can only imagine the panic as incurable, untreatable pestilence sweeps the globe.

PANG #6: Persecution

Those who come to faith in Jesus Christ during the Tribulation will face persecution, torture, beatings, trials, imprisonment, and even martyrdom.

"Then they will deliver you to tribulation, and will kill you, and you will be hated by all nations on account of My name. And at that time many will fall away and will deliver up one another and hate one another." (Matthew 24:9–10)

Mark's Gospel paints the same picture.

"But be on your guard; for they will deliver you to the courts, and you will be flogged in the synagogues, and you will stand before governors and kings for My sake, as a testimony to them." (Mark 13:9)

The world will show its venomous hatred for Christ in how it treats His servants.

PANG #7: False Prophets

The first birth pang is the rise of false Christs. Now the deception will escalate with the rise of false prophets who will delude and deceive the masses with their mesmerizing words. Jesus continues: "Many false prophets will arise, and will mislead many" (Matthew 24:11). Satan will flood the world with his evil emissaries.

> For such men are false apostles, deceitful workers, disguising themselves as apostles of Christ. And no wonder, for even Satan disguises himself as an angel of light. Therefore it is not surprising if his servants also disguise themselves as servants of righteousness. (2 Corinthians 11:13–15)

Then, out of this crowd of false prophets, one man will emerge. He will rise to the top of the hellish heap, the false prophet of Revelation 19:20. He is the beast out of the earth as described here:

> Then I saw another beast coming up out of the earth; and he had two horns like a lamb,

and he spoke as a dragon. And he exercises all the authority of the first beast in his presence. And he makes the earth and those who dwell in it to worship the first beast, whose fatal wound was healed. And he performs great signs, so that he even makes fire come down out of heaven to the earth in the presence of men. And he deceives those who dwell on the earth because of the signs which it was given him to perform in the presence of the beast, telling those who dwell on the earth to make an image to the beast who had the wound of the sword and has come to life. And it was given to him to give breath to the image of the beast, so that the image of the beast would even speak and cause as many as do not worship the image of the beast to be killed. And he causes all, the small and the great, and the rich and the poor, and the free men and the slaves, to be given a mark on their right hand or on their forehead, and he provides that no one will be able to buy or to sell, except the one who has the mark. (Revelation 13:11–17)

Together with Antichrist and Satan, the false prophet will round out the counterfeit, false trinity (Revelation 16:13).

The Unholy Trinity of the End Times

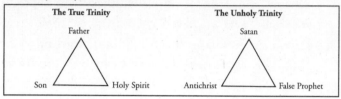

The false prophet will be the counterfeit counterpart of the Holy Spirit. Here are five ways the false prophet will counterfeit the ministry of the Holy Spirit.

HOLY SPIRIT	FALSE PROPHET
Points men to Christ	Points men to Antichrist
Instrument of divine revelation	Instrument of satanic revelation
Seals believers in God	Marks unbelievers with the number of Antichrist
Builds the body of Christ	Builds the empire of Antichrist
Enlightens men with the truth	Deceives men by miracles

Pang #8: Lawlessness Increased and Loss of Love

As the first birth pangs are about to give way to greater pain, Jesus adds, "Because lawlessness is increased, most people's love will grow cold" (Matthew 24:12).

During the Tribulation, lawlessness will increase exponentially. The world will become increasingly cold, harsh, and indifferent as the Tribulation wears on.

But even as things progress from bad to worse, genuine believers will display their faith in Christ by enduring to the end. "But the one who endures to the end, he will be saved" (Matthew 24:13).

This is not saying that people are saved because they endure. No one is ever saved because of their own efforts. But those who are true believers will endure. This doesn't mean that we can never waver, stumble, or fall. But it does mean that the true believer in Christ will never totally defect, renounce, apostatize, or depart from the faith.

What a comfort! Even in the worst circumstances, Christ will protect His people from turning away from Him.

Pang #9: Worldwide Preaching of the Gospel

This is the only positive sign that I can see in all this. It's like a breath of fresh air, the one gleam of light in the darkness. Jesus wants us to know that even during earth's darkest days God never ceases to extend His mercy to all who will respond to His gracious call.

But how will God spread the good news during the Tribulation? Through the supernaturally energized ministry of the 144,000 Jewish witnesses mentioned in Revelation 7:1–4:

> After this I saw four angels standing at the four corners of the earth, holding back the four winds of the earth, so that no wind would blow on the earth or on the sea or on any tree. And I saw another angel ascending from the rising of the sun, having the seal of the living God; and he cried out with a loud voice to the four angels to whom it was granted to harm the earth and the sea, saying, "Do not harm the earth or the sea or the trees until we have sealed the bond-servants of our God on their foreheads. And I heard the number of those who were sealed, one hundred and forty-four thousand sealed from every tribe of the sons of Israel."

And we know from Revelation 7:9–14 that the ministry of these 144,000 will reap a plentiful harvest.

There will be great revival during the Tribulation. God will save millions during this terrible time of judgment. Many of them will lose their lives. But their eternal souls will enter God's paradise,

> After these things I looked, and behold, a great multitude which no one could count, from every nation and all tribes and peoples and tongues, standing before the throne and before the Lamb, clothed in white robes, and palm branches were in their hands; and they cry out with a loud voice, saying, "Salvation to our God who sits on the throne, and to the Lamb." And all the angels were standing around the throne and around the elders and the four living creatures; and they fell on their faces before the throne and worshiped God, saying, "Amen, blessing and glory and wisdom and thanksgiving and honor and power and might, be to our God forever and ever. Amen." Then one of the elders answered, saying to me, "These who are clothed in the white robes, who are they, and where have they come from?" I said to him, "My lord, you know." And he said to me,

"These are the ones who come out of the great tribulation, and they have washed their robes and made them white in the blood of the Lamb. For this reason, they are before the throne of God; and they serve Him day and night in His temple; and He who sits on the throne will spread His tabernacle over them. They will hunger no longer, nor thirst anymore; nor will the sun beat down on them, nor any heat; for the Lamb in the center of the throne will be their shepherd, and will guide them to springs of the water of life; and God will wipe every tear from their eyes." (Revelation 7:9–17)

What grace!
What a Savior!

THE MINI APOCALYPSE

Remember, as I stated earlier, Jesus' sermon on the Mount of Olives is often called the "mini apocalypse" because it's a compact, concise overview of what we find expanded later in the entire book of Revelation. We see this parallel between Matthew 24–25 and Revelation 6–7 clearly at this point.

Matthew 24: 4–14	Revelation 6–7
False Christs (vv. 4–5)	The Rider on the White Horse (vv. 1–2)
Wars and Rumors of Wars (24:6–7)	The Rider on the Red Horse (vv. 3–4)
Famines and Earthquakes (24:7b)	The Rider on the Black Horse (vv. 5–6)
Famines and Plagues (v. 7; Luke 21:11)	The Rider on the Pale Horse (vv. 7–8)
Persecution and Martyrdom (vv. 9–10)	Martyrs (vv. 9–11)
Terrors and Great Cosmic Signs (Luke 21:11)	Terror (vv. 12–17)
Worldwide Preaching of the Gospel (v. 14)	Ministry of the 144,000 (7:1–8)

Remember, this is just the beginning of the time of Tribulation. These are just the initial birth pains. If they stopped right here, it would be hellish enough, but Jesus makes it abundantly clear that there's more to follow.

Much more.

All of this is merely a prelude of even greater horror to come. As the old saying goes, "It has to get worse before it gets better."

The birth pangs bring "tribulation," but "*great* tribulation" is still to come!

CHAPTER FOUR

THE SIGN

When Jesus' disciples asked Him about the end of the age, their question was very specific: "What will be the sign of Your coming, and of the end of the age." Notice they asked about the sign, singular. While Jesus proceeded to answer their question, He began by giving a kind of checklist of signs that would immediately portend His coming back to earth. But in Matthew 24:15, there is an important transition. A dramatic shift.

Jesus moves from general signs, events, and situations characterizing the end of the age to *the specific sign* that definitively signals the onset of the end.

And what is that singular sign?

Jesus called it the abomination of desolation.

THE PROPHET DANIEL

Jesus mentions the abomination of desolation in Matthew 24:15. But the terminology was not original with Jesus. He was referring to something the prophet Daniel had written about more than five hundred years earlier.

> Therefore when you see the ABOMINA-TION OF DESOLATION which was spoken of through Daniel the prophet, standing in the holy place (let the reader understand). (Matthew 24:15)

Daniel referred to the abomination of desolation three times in his great prophecy:

> And he will make a firm covenant with the many for one week, but in the middle of the week he will put a stop to sacrifice and grain offering; and on the wing of abominations will come one who makes desolate, even until a complete destruction, one that is decreed, is poured out on the one who makes desolate. (Daniel 9:27)

Forces from him will arise, desecrate the sanctuary fortress, and do away with the regular sacrifice. And they will set up the abomination of desolation. (Daniel 11:31)

From the time that the regular sacrifice is abolished and the abomination of desolation is set up, there will be 1,290 days. (Daniel 12:11)

Before we go any farther we need to define what is meant by the words "abomination of desolation." The word "abomination" refers to something that is absolutely detestable in the sight of God, primarily things connected with idolatry. The abomination of desolation, therefore, is an act of flagrant idolatry that will bring complete desolation, devastation, and ruin to the Jewish temple. Notice carefully that in all three uses of this term in Daniel it's associated with the temple and the sacrifices. It's an act of idolatry that will desolate the temple in Jerusalem.

The Sign

ANTIOCHUS AND THE
ABOMINATION

Daniel, writing in about 550 B.C., predicted that in the future a despicable person would arise who would desecrate the Jewish temple by setting up the abomination of desolation (Daniel 11:31). We know from the context of Daniel 11:21–31 that this was historically fulfilled in 167 B.C. by a wicked Syrian tyrant known as Antiochus IV, who ruled from 175–164 B.C.

He also was known as Antiochus "Epiphanes" ("manifest one" or "splendid one"). This was a brash claim to deity. However, the Jews, in a play on words, nicknamed him "Epimanes" ("mad man").

Antiochus was an aggressive persecutor of the Jewish people. He was personally responsible for the slaughter of tens of thousands of Jews. However, his most notorious act was his desecration of the Jewish temple. Antiochus offered a sow, an unclean animal in Judaism, as a sacrifice on the altar in the temple, thereby rendering the entire temple unclean. And as if this weren't brazen enough, in December 167 B.C. he set up an image of Zeus (which looked like himself!) in the temple, and erected an altar to Zeus right on the altar of burnt offering. As you can imagine, these heinous acts brought a sudden halt to the daily sacrifices to Yahweh in the Jewish temple, and for a time the temple was left desolate.[12]

This was the idolatrous abomination that brought desolation.

FAST FORWARD

While Antiochus did desolate the temple with his gross act of idolatry, it's clear that the abomination of desolation mentioned in Daniel 9:27 and 12:11 was not fulfilled by Antiochus. Two key points lead me to this conclusion. First, the abomination of desolation in Daniel 9:27 refers to the future Antichrist during the Tribulation period, not Antiochus. Antiochus never made a seven-year covenant with the Jewish people only to break it at the midpoint, as required by Daniel 9:27.

Second, in Matthew 24:15, Jesus clearly said that the abomination of desolation was still future in His day, almost two hundred years after Antiochus's monstrous act.

Therefore, the desecrating act of Antiochus merely served as a foreshadowing, or "type" of the final desolation of the Jewish temple by Antichrist. The wicked act of Antiochus will be repeated in the end times as the trigger for the Great Tribulation.

The parenthetical words of Jesus at the very end of Matthew 24:15 are very instructive. "Let the reader understand." This statement seems to indicate a meaning that would speak to a future generation of readers who would actually witness the unfolding of these events.

According to Daniel 9:27, for at least some of the time during the first half of the Tribulation, the Jewish people, under their covenant with Antichrist, will offer sacrifices in the rebuilt temple.

However, at the midpoint of the seven-year Tribulation period that will all change. Daniel 9:27 says, "but in the middle of the week he will put a stop to sacrifice and grain offering; and on the wing of abominations will come one who makes desolate, even until a complete destruction, one that is decreed, is poured out on the one who makes desolate."

At this point, the Antichrist will break his covenant with Israel and commit this detestable act that Daniel and Jesus refer to as the abomination of desolation. But what exactly will happen?

We know that it will be very similar to what

Antiochus did over two thousand years ago, but what exactly will this future abomination of desolation by Antichrist look like?

ANTICHRIST'S ABOMINATION

The first reference to the abomination of desolation in Daniel 9:27 links it with Antichrist's breaking of the covenant with Israel and the temple. The phrase "on the wing of abominations" refers to the pinnacle of the temple, emphasizing the idea of an overspreading influence. In other words, what begins at the temple will spread to other places.[13] The abomination of desolation, then, is an idol or image that desolates the temple and spreads out from there to the world.

According to Scripture, two main elements or phases are involved in the future abomination of desolation. The first phase is described for us in 2 Thessalonians 2:3–4:

> Let no one in any way deceive you, for it will not come unless the apostasy comes first, and the man of lawlessness is revealed, the son of destruction, who opposes and exalts himself above every so-called god or object of worship,

so that he takes his seat in the temple of God, displaying himself as being God.

In his initial takeover of Jerusalem, Antichrist will sit in the very holy of holies in the temple declaring to the world that he is God, thus establishing the final false religion that he will impose on the entire world. The second aspect of the abomination of desolation is described in Revelation 13:11–15:

And I saw another beast coming up out of the earth; and he had two horns like a lamb, and he spoke as a dragon. And he exercises all the authority of the first beast in his presence. And he makes all the earth and those who dwell in it to worship the first beast, whose fatal wound was healed. And he performs great signs, so that he even makes fire come down out of heaven to the earth in the presence of men. And he deceives those who dwell on the earth because of the signs which it was given him to perform in the presence of the beast, telling those who dwell on the earth to make an image to the beast who had the wound of the sword and has come to life. And there was given to him to give breath to the image of the beast, that the image of the beast might even speak and cause as many as do not worship the image of the beast to be killed.

The Antichrist's right-hand man, the false prophet, will be given the authority to do great signs and wonders, deceiving people into worshiping the beast. His greatest deception will be the construction of an image or likeness of the Antichrist that will come alive.

This image will be placed in the holy of holies in the temple in Jerusalem, to carry forward the abomination of desolation. Jerusalem will serve as a great world center for the worship of Antichrist, and the temple will serve as the center of worship, with the living image standing in its inner precinct. All the earth will be required to worship the beast and his image, or to face death.

The two phases of the abomination of desolation, therefore, will be (1) the declaration of the deity of the Antichrist in the holy of holies in the temple at the midpoint of the Tribulation, followed by (2) the setting up of his image in the same place. This condition will go on for the final 1,260 days or three-and-a-half years of the Tribulation period.[14]

The abomination of desolation, perpetrated by the Antichrist, is the event that commences the final three-and-a-half years of the age. It's the event that signals the onset of the time period Jesus called the "great tribulation."

HEAD FOR THE HILLS

The appearance of the abomination of desolation will serve as *the* sign to those living in the end times that the end of the age is near. Times of unimaginable danger and persecution will be at hand. Therefore, Jesus issues a sober warning to those living in Judea at that time.

> "Then those who are in Judea must flee to the mountains. Whoever is on the housetop must not go down to get the things out that are in his house. Whoever is in the field must not turn back to get his cloak. But woe to those who are pregnant and to those who are nursing babies in those days! But pray that your flight will not be in the winter, or on a Sabbath. For then there

will be a great tribulation, such as has not occurred since the beginning of the world until now, nor ever will. Unless those days had been cut short, no life would have been saved; but for the sake of the elect those days will be cut short." (Matthew 24:16–22)

Interestingly, Jesus never spoke words like this at any other time. He consistently called upon His followers to stand firm even in the face of hatred and hostility. But the circumstances in the Great Tribulation will call for urgent action. The Jews living in Israel during the Tribulation are called upon to flee without the slightest hesitation or delay. Every second will count. Antichrist will be hot on their heels as his three-and-a-half-year reign of terror against the Jewish people begins.

READY TO REBUILD?

Of course, for the Antichrist to establish his abomination of desolation in the temple there must be a temple in Jerusalem. The Bible doesn't tell us specifically how the temple will be rebuilt. We don't know what conditions will come about to make the temple a reality. But one thing is sure—it will be rebuilt in Jerusalem just as God's Word predicts! And there are some amazing preparations going on in Jerusalem today for the rebuilding of the third Jewish temple.

For example, the Temple Institute in Jerusalem is working vigorously to construct the objects and utensils needed for renewed worship in the third temple, including the Menorah of pure gold, the pure gold crown worn by the high priest, firepans and shovels, the mitzraq (vessel used to transport the blood of sacrificial offerings), the copper laver, linen garments of the priests, stone vessels to store the ashes of the red heifer, and so on. There are also ongoing efforts to produce an unblemished red heifer to fulfill the purification requirements of Numbers 19:1–10.

Randall Price, the foremost evangelical authority on the temple, concludes his excellent, up-to-date book on the temple with these words:

> What does this say to you and me? It says that not only have the Jews already begun the ascent to their goal, but they are only one step away from accomplishing it!... We live...on the brink of the rebuilding effort, and with it the

beginning of the fulfillment of the prophecies that will move the world rapidly to see as a reality the coming Last Days Temple.[15]

Two of the key things that had to happen for the temple to be rebuilt have already occurred. The Jews are back in their land and they have control of Jerusalem. All that remains is for them to reassume sovereignty over the Temple Mount.

When this occurs the temple will be rebuilt, and Antichrist's desolation of it won't be far behind.

CHAPTER FIVE

THE GREAT TRIBULATION

Jesus told us many things in His great discourse from the Mount of Olives, but one point comes through loud and clear in His answer to His disciples. This world is not going to become a better place.

Times of almost unbelievable difficulty are on the horizon. Jesus said that the end of the age will be a totally unique time of terror. Nothing in all of world history will even compare to what is coming. Jesus made it crystal clear.

> "For then there will be a great tribulation, such as has not occurred since the beginning of the world until now, nor ever will." (Matthew 24:21)

Now that's really saying something! Stop and think about some of the terrible times in world history:

The Black Plague in Europe

The Thirty Years' War

World War II

Hitler and the Holocaust

Stalin's Reign of Terror

The Killing Fields of Cambodia

Two things will make the Great Tribulation worse than any other time of trouble in world history. First, the terror and destruction of the Great Tribulation will not be limited to a few locations. The entire world will be engulfed. Second, most of the trouble in the world up to this point is the result of the wrath of man and the wrath of Satan. However, in the Great Tribulation, God Himself will be pouring out His unmitigated wrath on a sinful, rebellious world. And it will be unlike anything the world has ever witnessed.

If the first half of the Tribulation is labor, then the great Tribulation is *hard* labor. It's the final three-and-a-half years of hard labor for planet earth. Jesus doesn't give many of the details of this time of terror. He just says that it will be the worst time in all of human history.

For more details we have to turn to the book of Revelation.

TRUMPETS AND BOWLS

As we saw earlier, the first half of the Tribulation in Matthew 24:4–14 is paralleled by the seal judgments in Revelation 6–7. Likewise the Great Tribulation of this age, in Matthew 24:21–28, is paralleled and greatly amplified by the events that are graphically described in Revelation 8–16: the seven trumpets and seven bowls.

Here's a brief overview of these trumpet and bowl judgments that will be poured out during the Great Tribulation.

SEVEN TRUMPET JUDGMENTS OF REVELATION 8–11	
First Trumpet (8:7)	Bloody Hail and Fire: One-Third of Vegetation Destroyed
Second Trumpet (8:8–9)	Fireball from Heaven: One-Third of Oceans Polluted
Third Trumpet (8:10–11)	Falling Star: One-Third of Fresh Water Polluted
Fourth Trumpet (8:12)	Darkness: One-Third of Sun, Moon and Stars Darkened
Fifth Trumpet (9:1–12)	Demonic Invasion: Torment
Sixth Trumpet (9:13–21)	Demonic Army: One-Third of Mankind Killed
Seventh Trumpet (11:15–19)	The Kingdom: The Announcement of Christ's Reign

The seven trumpet judgments will be unleashed during the main part of the Great Tribulation. And then, just before the end, the final seven judgments, the bowls, will be poured out in rapid succession. Like the blows of a trip hammer the labor pains will reach a fever pitch that will bring the world to the brink of total destruction.

SEVEN BOWL JUDGMENTS OF REVELATION 16	
First Bowl (v. 2)	Upon the earth: Sores on the Worshipers of the Antichrist
Second Bowl (v. 3)	Upon the Seas: Turned to Blood
Third Bowl (vv. 4–7)	Upon the Fresh Water: Turned to Blood
Fourth Bowl (vv. 8–9)	Upon the Sun: Intense, Scorching Heat
Fifth Bowl (vv. 10–11)	Upon the Antichrist's Kingdom: Darkness and Pain
Sixth Bowl (vv. 12–16)	Upon the River Euphrates: Armageddon
Seventh Bowl (vv. 17–21)	Upon the Air: Earthquakes and Hail

Now you can see why Jesus says it will be the worst time in human history. God will pour out His wrath on the entire world.

WILL MAN SURVIVE?

Jesus' statement about the severity of the Great Tribulation leaves one wondering how anyone could survive. We know from Zechariah 13:8 that as many as two-thirds of the world's Jewish population will be slain during Antichrist's reign of terror.

In the fourth seal judgment, one-fourth of earth's population is killed, and in the sixth trumpet judgment another one-third is destroyed. That's one-half of the world's population in just two of the Tribulation judgments. Then, as the bowls of wrath are poured out in Revelation 16 in rapid succession, the total annihilation of the human race will seem imminent.

Our Lord anticipated that we would someday ask this question so He has already given us His solution to the problem.

> "For then there will be a great tribulation, such as has not occurred since the beginning of the world until now, nor ever will. Unless those days had been cut short, no life would have been saved; but for the sake of the elect those days will be cut short." (Matthew 24:21–22)

This passage doesn't mean that the Lord will shorten the Tribulation period to make it less than the time He intended. It also doesn't mean that the days will be less than twenty four hours.

These encouraging words simply mean that the Lord will not allow the Tribulation to go on indefinitely. He will cut it short by ending it at the divinely appointed time. The Lord ends it when He does for the sake of those who have been saved during this time and are undergoing terrible suffering.

The Lord assures us that there will be many people who will survive the horrors of the Tribulation. All these people will be gathered together for judgment when Christ returns, and the righteous will enter the millennial kingdom while the lost will be cast into eternal fire (Matthew 25:31–46).

THE SAVIOR COMES

The only thing that can save the world is the coming of Jesus Christ. Praise God that we have the promise of His return to redeem this world.

Let's see what Jesus had to say about that great day when He will split the sky, riding on a milk-white stallion as King of kings and Lord of lords.

THE KING IS COMING!

Sixty-six percent of Americans, including a third of those who admit they never attend church, say they believe Jesus will return to earth someday
U.S. NEWS AND WORLD REPORT, 1997

Twenty percent of Americans said they believe the Second Coming will occur sometime around the year 2000.
DALLAS MORNING NEWS, 1998

The Great Tribulation begins with the abomination of desolation. It climaxes with the Second Coming of Jesus Christ. Matthew 24:29 says, "But immediately after the tribulation of those days THE SUN WILL BE DARKENED, AND THE

MOON WILL NOT GIVE ITS LIGHT, AND THE STARS WILL FALL from the sky, and the powers of the heavens will be shaken."

The Second Coming of Christ will bring this present age to a screeching halt. Truly, it will be the "end of the age."

But what will happen when Jesus comes? What will it be like? How and where will He come?

Thankfully, we aren't left to our own imaginations about these issues. Jesus answered these questions for us very clearly.

"So if they say to you, 'Behold, He is in the wilderness,' do not go out, or, 'Behold, He is in the inner rooms,' do not believe them. For just as the lightning comes from the east and flashes even to the west, so will the coming of the Son of Man be. Wherever the corpse is, there the vultures will gather. But immediately after the tribulation of those days THE SUN WILL BE DARKENED, AND THE MOON WILL NOT GIVE ITS LIGHT, AND THE STARS WILL FALL from the sky, and the powers of the heavens will be shaken. And then the sign of the

Son of Man will appear in the sky, and then all the tribes of the earth will mourn, and they will see the SON OF MAN COMING ON THE CLOUDS OF THE SKY with power and great glory. And He will send forth His angels with A GREAT TRUMPET and THEY WILL GATHER TOGETHER His elect from the four winds, from one end of the sky to the other." (Matthew 24:26–31)

How Will Jesus Return?

There are ten key words that vividly, effectively describe how Jesus Himself told us He will return to the earth at His Second Coming.

Jesus Is Coming Personally

Jesus will not send someone else on His behalf. He Himself will return.

Jesus called Himself the Son of Man about eighty times in the Gospels. When Jesus refers to the coming of the Son of Man He means Himself.

The personal nature of Christ's coming is confirmed in other passages in the New Testament as well.

And as they were gazing intently into the sky while He was going, behold, two men in white clothing stood beside them. They also said, Men of Galilee, why do you stand looking into the sky? This Jesus, who has been taken up from you into heaven, will come in just the same way as you have watched Him go into heaven. (Acts 1:10–11)

"Yes, I am coming quickly." (Revelation 22:20)

Jesus Is Coming Literally

The coming of Jesus is not a spiritual or symbolic coming. It is *literal* and *real.* He came literally the first time to Bethlehem; He will come literally again.

And I saw heaven opened, and behold, a white horse, and He who sat on it is called Faithful and True, and in righteousness He judges and wages war. His eyes are a flame of fire, and on His head are many diadems; and He has a name written on Him which no one knows except Himself.

He is clothed with a robe dipped in blood, and His name is called The Word of God. (Revelation 19:11–13)

Jesus Is Coming Visibly

Jesus is not coming secretly. He will not come back incognito. His coming will not be hidden or easy to miss. It will be open and visible to all the world. No one on earth will miss it.

"Then if anyone says to you, 'Behold, here is the Christ,' or 'There He is,' do not believe him. For false Christs and false prophets will arise and will show great signs and wonders, so as to mislead, if possible, even the elect. Behold, I have told you in advance. So if they say to you, 'Behold, He is in the wilderness,' do not go out, or, 'Behold, He is in the inner rooms,' do not believe them. For just as the lightning comes from the east and flashes even to the west, so will the coming of the Son of Man be." (Matthew 24:23–27)

BEHOLD, HE IS COMING WITH THE CLOUDS, and every eye will see Him, even those who pierced Him; and all the tribes of the earth will mourn over Him. So it is to be. Amen. (Revelation 1:7)

Jesus Is Coming Suddenly

The Second Coming of Jesus will be sudden. It won't occur over a long, drawn-out period or in a bunch of small stages. It will come suddenly like flashing lightning in the night (Matthew 24:27).

Jesus Is Coming Unexpectedly

Jesus is not only coming suddenly, but He is coming unexpectedly upon an unprepared world. His return is compared to the coming of a thief. No one ever expects a thief to come to his house. In the same way the unbelieving world will be caught totally by surprise.

"Therefore be on the alert, for you do not know which day your Lord is coming. But be sure of this, that if the head of the house had known at what time of the night the thief was coming, he would have been on the alert and would not have allowed his house to be broken into. For this reason you also must be ready; for the Son of Man is coming at an hour when you do not think He will." (Matthew 24:42–44)

This same imagery appears elsewhere in the New Testament.

For you yourselves know full well that the day of the Lord will come just like a thief in the night. (1 Thessalonians 5:2)

So remember what you have received and heard; and keep it, and repent. Therefore if you do not wake up, I will come like a thief, and you will not know at what hour I will come to you. (Revelation 3:3)

"Behold, I am coming like a thief. Blessed is the one who stays awake and keeps his clothes, so that he will not walk about naked and men will not see his shame." (Revelation 16:15)

Also, as in the days of Noah when the flood water caught them totally unaware, Jesus' return will catch many people totally unprepared:

> "For the coming of the Son of Man will be just like the days of Noah. For as in those days before the flood they were eating and drinking, marrying and giving in marriage, until the day that Noah entered the ark, and they did not understand until the flood came and took them all away; so will the coming of the Son of Man be." (Matthew 24:37–39).

Jesus Is Coming Dramatically

Jesus' coming will be attended by dramatic signs in the heavens. These cosmic signs will serve as the final harbingers of His coming. Christ's return will be the most dramatic event in human history.

> "But immediately after the tribulation of those days THE SUN WILL BE DARKENED, AND THE MOON WILL NOT GIVE ITS LIGHT, AND THE STARS WILL FALL from the sky,

and the powers of the heavens will be shaken."
(Matthew 24:29)

"There will be signs in sun and moon and
stars, and on the earth dismay among nations,
in perplexity at the roaring of the sea and the
waves, men fainting from fear and the expectation of the things which are coming upon
the world; for the powers of the heavens will
be shaken." (Luke 21:25–26)

Jesus Is Coming Gloriously

In Matthew 24:30, Jesus speaks of one final sign that
He is returning: "And then the sign of the Son of Man
will appear in the sky, and then all the tribes of the
earth will mourn, and they will see the SON OF
MAN COMING ON THE CLOUDS OF THE SKY
with power and great glory."

Many have wondered what this "sign of the Son of
Man" might be. While there are several possible
answers, I believe the best view is to simply see this as
Jesus Himself. The final sign of His coming will be His

appearance in the sky where every eye will see Him. It is the ultimate sign of all signs—the dramatic appearance of Jesus Himself.

Jesus Is Coming Triumphantly

Jesus will return as King of kings and Lord of lords. He is coming back to take over!

All the armies of the earth will be amassed to meet him, yet amazingly, no struggle is recorded. All Jesus will have to do to completely vanquish His enemies is speak the words "Drop Dead!" (2 Thessalonians 1:9)

> And I saw the beast and the kings of the earth and their armies assembled to make war against Him...and the beast was seized, and with him the false prophet who performed the signs in his presence, by which he deceived those who had received the mark of the beast and those who worshiped his image; these two were thrown alive into the lake of fire which burns with brimstone. And the rest were killed with the sword which came from the mouth of Him who sat on the horse, and all the birds were filled with their flesh. (Revelation 19:19–21)

J. C. Ryle beautifully pictures the stark contrast between Christ's first coming in humility and His Second Coming in triumph.

The second personal coming of Christ will be as different as possible from the first. He came the first time as "a man of sorrows, and familiar with suffering" (Isaiah 53:3): he was born in the manger of Bethlehem, in lowliness and humiliation; he took the very nature of a servant, and was despised and not esteemed; he was betrayed into the hands of wicked men, condemned by an unjust judgment, mocked, flogged, crowned with thorns and at last crucified between two thieves. He will come the second time as the King of all the earth, with royal majesty: the princes and great men of this world will themselves stand before his throne to receive an eternal sentence: before him every mouth shall be silenced, and every knee bow, and every tongue shall confess that Jesus Christ is Lord! May we all remember this![16]

Jesus Is Coming Finally

The return of Jesus will not just be sudden and unexpected; it will be final. There will be no second chances. No appeal. There will be no time for repentance or a change of mind. Everyone will be taken exactly as they are. When Christ returns there will be an immediate, eternal separation and division of the redeemed from the lost.

> "For as in those days before the flood they were eating and drinking, marrying and giving in marriage, until the day that Noah entered the ark, and they did not understand until the flood came and took them all away; so will the coming of the Son of Man be. Then there will be two men in the field; one will be taken and one will be left. Two women will be grinding at the mill; one will be taken and one will be left." (Matthew 24:38–41)

The fate of all men on earth at that time will be sealed at that moment. And for the lost, Jesus will come upon them like a thief and take everything they have.

Jesus Is Coming Certainly

This is the best part of all. Jesus says, "Heaven and earth will pass away, but My words will not pass away" (Matthew 24:35). Jesus doesn't want any doubt about it. His coming is sure. It's a done deal.

Nothing is more clearly stated in the Bible. The emphasis on the Second Coming and its absolute certainty are seen in the following Scriptural statistics.

1. Jesus' return to planet earth is explicitly referred to 1,845 times in the Bible (1,527 times in the Old Testament and 318 times in the New Testament).
2. The Second Coming is mentioned in twenty-three of twenty-seven New Testament books. Three of the remaining four books are one-chapter books (Philemon, 2 John, 3 John), and the book of Galatians implies the Second Coming in verse 4 of chapter 1.
3. There are 260 chapters in the New Testament and 318 references to the Second Coming of Christ.
4. The Second Coming of Christ is mentioned eight times for every one reference to His first coming.
5. For every single mention of the Atonement in the Bible, the Second Coming is mentioned twice.

6. The first recorded prophecy concerned the Second Coming. In the days before the flood, Enoch spoke of the Lord's coming to judge the earth (Jude 14).

7. The final prophecy ever given deals with the Second Coming (Rev. 22:20). Six times in the book of Revelation we hear Jesus say, "I come quickly," three times in the final chapter alone (22:7, 12, 20).

8. Men are exhorted over fifty times to be ready for the return of Jesus.

9. Jesus Christ Himself refers to His return twenty-one times.

10. Angels believe and testify that Christ is coming back. When He ascended to heaven, angels stated that He would return just as He left (Acts 1:9–11).[17]

Make no mistake, Jesus is coming back just as He promised!

WHY WILL JESUS RETURN?

When the seven-year Tribulation has run its course, "after the tribulation of those days," Jesus will come in great power and glory to judge the wicked and to gather the elect of Israel, and the Gentile nations who have survived the Tribulation, and usher them into His one-thousand-year Kingdom.

> "But when the Son of Man comes in His glory, and all the angels with Him, then He will sit on His glorious throne. All the nations will be gathered before Him; and He will separate them from one another, as the shepherd separates the sheep from the goats; and He will put the sheep on His right, and the goats on the left." (Matthew 25:31–33)

> For I do not want you, brethren, to be uninformed of this mystery—so that you will not be wise in your own estimation—that a partial hardening has happened to Israel until the fullness of the Gentiles has come in; and so all Israel will be saved; just as it is written, "THE DELIVERER WILL COME FROM ZION, HE WILL REMOVE UNGODLINESS FROM JACOB. THIS IS MY COVENANT WITH THEM, WHEN I TAKE AWAY THEIR SINS." (Romans 11:25–27)

WHERE WILL JESUS RETURN?

The Bible is clear that Jesus will return to the same place from which He left, the Mount of Olives. Three key passages help identify this as the place of His return.

1. Zechariah 14:4 addresses the Second Coming of Christ. "And in that day His feet will stand on the Mount of Olives, which is in front of Jerusalem on the east; and the Mount of Olives will be split in its middle from east to west by a very large valley, so that half of the mountain will move toward the north and the other half toward the south."

2. Jesus gave His great prophetic discourse, which gave the signs of His coming, from the Mount of Olives in Matthew 24–25.

3. When Jesus ascended to heaven from the Mount of Olives in Acts 1:9–11, the angels said that He would return just as He had left. While this could simply mean that He will return in the same manner, it also seems to carry the idea that He will return to the same place from which He left.

WHAT ABOUT THE RAPTURE?

I know what you are probably thinking at this point. What about the Rapture? Is the Rapture the same thing as the Second Coming? Did Jesus have anything to say about the Rapture? Will church-age believers have to go through the Great Tribulation?

Those are very important questions, which many people today are wrestling with. So, let's see what Jesus had to say about the relationship between the Tribulation, the Rapture, and the church.

WILL THE CHURCH GO THROUGH THE TRIBULATION?

O ne of the most debated issues in end-time study is the timing of the Rapture. All people who believe the Bible believe in a Rapture. Remember, the Rapture is that future event when all who have personally trusted in Jesus Christ as their Savior, the living and the dead, will be caught up to meet the Lord in the air and go with Him back up to heaven.

The big issue is not whether there will be a Rapture, but when it will occur.

In this book I don't have space to go into extended detail concerning all the various views on the Rapture's timing. This chart and timeline should help in giving a broad overview of where people are on this issue.

1	The Pretribulational Rapture	The Rapture will occur before the tribulation period begins.
2	The Midtribulational Rapture	The Rapture will occur at the midpoint of the Tribulation.
3	The Posttribulational Rapture	The Rapture will occur at the end of the Tribulation right before the second coming of Christ back to earth; believers will be raptured up to meet Christ in the air and then will return immediately with Him back to the earth.
4	The Partial Rapture	Faithful, devoted believers will be raptured before the Tribulation, but the rest of believers will be left to go through the purging of the Tribulation.
5	The Prewrath Rapture	The Rapture will occur about three-fourths (five-and-a-half years) of the way through the Tribulation, when the wrath of God begins to be poured out on the earth at the seventh seal.

Various Views of the Timing of the Rapture

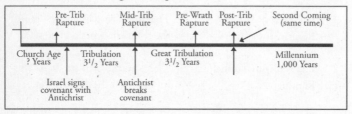

The two main views of the timing of the Rapture are the pre-trib view and the post-trib position. Those who hold to a post-tribulational Rapture appeal strongly to Matthew 24 for support. Let's examine the four most common arguments post-tribulationists use and see what Jesus Himself said about the Rapture and the Tribulation.

THE GATHERING OF THE ELECT

In Matthew 24:31, Jesus refers to the "elect" who are on earth while the Tribulation is going on. In this verse He says: "And He will send forth His angels with A GREAT TRUMPET and THEY WILL GATHER TOGETHER His elect from the four winds, from one end of the sky to the other."

A very natural question for us to ask is, who are these people? If the church is raptured to heaven before the Tribulation, then who are all these "elect" believers on earth when Jesus returns? Post-tribula-tionists say that these people must be church-age believers who are going through the Great Tribulation. And when Jesus comes He will gather His people to Himself by rapturing them to heaven.

But the answer to this question is really quite simple in the context. The gathered elect are Jewish believers who have trusted Jesus as their Messiah during the time of the Tribulation and have then been scattered by Antichrist's persecution.

In Matthew 23:39, just before He began His great end-times discourse, Jesus said that the Jewish people would not see Him again until they said, "Blessed is He who comes in the name of the Lord!" This sets the immediate context for the all of Matthew 24. During the Tribulation period, God will use this time of terror to bring many Jews to faith in Jesus as Messiah. He will bring them to cry out to Jesus in faith, "Blessed is He who comes in the name of the Lord." And only when this occurs will Jesus return. The entire Tribulation can then be viewed as a great prelude to the redemption of the Jewish people (Romans 11:26). At the end of the Tribulation, Jesus will gather them to enter into the Messianic kingdom.

Of course, God will also use this time to save many Gentiles. The whole picture of the sheep and the goats in Matthew 25:31–46 is a judgment scene of saved and lost Gentiles who have survived the Great Tribulation. The sheep are saved Gentiles who reveal their right relationship to Christ by their works.

WHY THE WARNING?

Another point that post-tribulationists make is, why would Jesus tell His followers all about the future Tribulation if we aren't even going to be in it?

Again the answer is manifest. God often warns His people concerning future times of judgment that they will not be a part of. For instance, God told Abraham about His destruction of Sodom and Gomorrah even though Abraham was totally exempt from the judgment (Genesis 18). But what God shared with Abraham motivated him to pray earnestly to God for mercy.

Genesis 18:17 is a touching verse concerning God's intimate relationship with His people. God said, "Shall I hide from Abraham what I am about to do?" The answer of course was no. God took Abraham into His confidence and revealed to him what was going to happen.

Likewise, God shares the future with us even though we will not personally experience His wrath. He does this for many reasons: to show us His sovereign control, to warn us of the dire consequences of sin, and to motivate us to evangelize and pray for those who don't know Him.

WHEN THE TRUMPET SOUNDS!

Matthew 24:31 says that when Jesus returns, "He will send forth His angels with a great trumpet." Posttribulationists maintain that this blowing of the trumpet is the same as the sounding of the trumpet mentioned in classic Rapture passages such as 1 Corinthians 15:52 and 1 Thessalonians 4:16.

The difficulty here is that, as we have seen, the elect in this context are Jewish believers; whereas, in 1 Corinthians 15 and 1 Thessalonians the New Testament church is in view. For this reason, the trumpets in these passages seem to be clearly distinct from one another.

LEFT BEHIND!

One of the most sobering statements of Jesus is found in Matthew 24:39–41:

"People didn't realize what was going to happen until the Flood came and swept them all away. That is the way it will be when the Son of Man comes. Two men will be working together in the field; one will be taken, the other left. Two women will be grinding flour at the mill; one will be taken, the other left." (NLT)

It's obvious that the context of these verses is the end of the Tribulation. This separation occurs in conjunction with Jesus' Second Coming. At that time, some are taken and some are left behind. So then, does this mean that the Rapture will occur at the end of the Tribulation?

I don't think so. I don't believe these verses are dealing with the Rapture at all. Notice the context. Jesus has just said that, in Noah's day, the flood came and took all the ungodly away in judgment. Then, by analogy, He says the same thing will occur when Jesus returns. Jesus will take the ungodly away to judgment while the righteous are "left behind" to enter Christ's glorious kingdom.

John Walvoord explains the meaning of this passage clearly.

Because at the Rapture believers will be taken out of the world, some have confused this with the Rapture of the church. Here, however, the situation is the reverse. The one who is left, is left to enter the kingdom; the one who is taken, is taken in judgment. This is in keeping with the illustration of the time of Noah when the ones taken away are the unbelievers.[18]

THE RAPTURE VERSUS THE SECOND COMING

It's clear from Matthew 24 that the Second Coming of Jesus back to earth will be heralded by many signs. In fact, it cannot occur until all these signs are fulfilled.

However, the imminence of Christ's coming permeates the pages of the New Testament. The inspired writers convey the unmistakable idea that we should be ready for Christ's coming at any moment. Expectations were very high. The New Testament breathes with an eager expectancy of Christ's coming. The New Testament consistently conveys the sense that it could happen at any moment, with no signs or warning.

Here is just a sampling of verses that yield this hope.

The night is almost gone, and the day is near. Therefore let us lay aside the deeds of darkness and put on the armor of light. Let us behave properly as in the day, not in carousing and drunkenness, not in sexual promiscuity and sensuality, not in strife and jealousy. But put on the Lord Jesus Christ, and make no provision for the flesh in regard to its lusts. (Romans 13:12–14)

When Christ, who is our life, is revealed, then you also will be revealed with Him in glory. (Colossians 3:4)

In the future there is laid up for me the crown of righteousness, which the Lord, the righteous Judge, will award to me on that day; and not only to me, but also to all who have loved His appearing. (2 Timothy 4:8)

Looking for the blessed hope and the appearing of the glory of our great God and Savior, Christ Jesus. (Titus 2:13)

The end of all things is near; therefore, be of sound judgment and sober spirit for the purpose of prayer. (1 Peter 4:7)

And when the Chief Shepherd appears, you will receive the unfading crown of glory. (1 Peter 5:4)

Now, little children, abide in Him, so that when He appears, we may have confidence and not shrink away from Him in shame at His coming. (1 John 2:28)

As you can see, this poses a serious dilemma. Jesus said clearly that His coming would be preceded by many specific, discernible signs—events that must occur before He can come. Yet the New Testament also presents Christ's coming as a signless, any-moment event that His followers can rightly expect at any time. How can both of these teachings be true at the same time?

The only way, or at least the best, most biblical way, to solve this dilemma is to pose a two-stage or two-phase coming of Christ. Both a Rapture and a return—a signless coming of Christ for His saints at the Rapture before the Tribulation, and a coming of Christ with His saints at the end of the Tribulation after all the signs in Matthew 24:4–28 have been literally fulfilled.

Jesus actually taught both the Rapture and the return. In Matthew 24, on the Wednesday before His death, He taught clearly about His return to earth, preceded by great signs. But the very next night, the night before His death, during His Upper Room discourse, in John 14:1–3, Jesus told His followers that one day He would come again to take them to be with Him in His Father's house.

> "Do not let your heart be troubled; believe in God, believe also in Me. In My Father's house are many dwelling places; if it were not so, I would have told you; for I go to prepare a place for you. If I go and prepare a place for you, I will come again and receive you to Myself, that where I am, there you may be also." (John 14:1–3)

I believe this event Jesus spoke of is the Rapture. And notice carefully that Jesus didn't mention any signs for this event. It is a signless event when Jesus comes for His saints. Jesus made this statement to His disciples at this critical juncture to bring them comfort and hope in their troubled state of mind.

Jesus also intended for this great statement to bring comfort to our hearts in troubled times as well. He is coming for us to take us to be with Him. But how much comfort will it be if we have to go through the Great Tribulation before He can come? Not very much I'm afraid. After all, Jesus said "Let not your heart be troubled," not "Let your heart be troubled." I don't know about you, but the thought of enduring the horror of the Tribulation before getting raptured isn't too reassuring to me.

I believe Jesus taught a pre-trib Rapture.

ARE YOU READY?

I am solidly convinced that the pre-tribulational Rapture view is the most consistent, biblical view. However, the key issue for all of us is not what view we hold but whether our view holds us. Does it change the way we live? Does it spur us on to live for Christ as we wait for Him to come?

CHAPTER EIGHT

READY OR NOT!

A young pastor once commented to a former seminary professor that he didn't preach on prophecy because "prophecy distracts people from the present." His former professor replied, "Then there is certainly a lot of distraction in the Scriptures!"

Bible prophecy was never given to distract people from the present. To the contrary, it was always related in some way to the here and now. Every time Jesus discussed the future, He always connected it powerfully to the present. His teaching about the future always placed demands upon His hearers for their lives in the present tense.

Matthew 24–25 is no exception. Jesus spends forty-one verses setting forth the outline of earth's final days (Matthew 24:1–41), and then spends fifty-six verses (Matthew 24:42–25:46) applying these truths to our daily lives. This makes it abundantly clear that Jesus was not just some pie-in-the-sky prophet.

Jesus consummated His apocalyptic sermon with several riveting parables to call His listeners to be ready, alert, and busy when He comes.

In the context of Matthew 24, these parables speak directly to those who will be alive on earth during the Great Tribulation, awaiting the Second Coming of Christ. We need to remember that this is their true interpretation and application. However, we too are awaiting Christ's coming at the Rapture. So, we can legitimately apply the principles in these parables to our lives as well, as we await our heavenly Bridegroom to come and catch His bride away.

Let's take a look at three of the key parables that Jesus gave to His followers to bring His teaching on the end times down to earth, where their sandals met the road.

THE PARABLE OF THE TWO SERVANTS

"Who then is the faithful and sensible slave whom his master put in charge of his household to give them their food at the proper time? Blessed is that slave whom his master finds so doing when he comes. Truly I say to you that he will put him in charge of all his possessions. But if that evil slave says in his heart, 'My master is not coming for a long time,' and begins to beat his fellow slaves and eat and drink with drunkards; the master of that slave will come on a day when he does not expect him and at an hour which he does not know, and will cut him in pieces and assign him a place with the hypocrites; in that place there will be weeping and gnashing of teeth." (Matthew 24:45–51)

The metaphor in the parable is very plain.

Jesus is the master who owns everything. Life is pictured as a stewardship in which the Master hands over His possessions to slaves to oversee and manage. These possessions represent all the gifts, abilities, opportunities, and resources that Christ entrusts to men.

The sensible slave represents a true believer in Christ who reveals his attitude of faith and love for the Master by His faithful, conscientious attitude of service. The evil slave portrays an unbeliever who shows what he really is by his reckless, selfish living.

I believe the key verse in this parable is verse 48: "But if that evil slave says in his heart, 'My master is not coming for a long time.'"

The real heart attitude of the evil slave is exposed. He believes he has plenty of time. He has no real expectation that the master will return. Therefore, he's self-indulgent, self-absorbed. He uses other people.

Life Lessons from the Parable of the Two Servants

1. Jesus may come much more quickly than we expect.
2. Jesus will come unexpectedly and catch the unbelieving totally off guard (v. 50).
3. Unbelievers are devoid of any real anticipation of Christ's return.
4. Unbelievers have a false sense of security.
5. Unsaved people live for themselves (v. 49).
6. True believers reveal their love for the Master by their faithful, diligent lives.
7. Hell is an unimaginable place of sorrow, loss, and torment (24:51).

Which slave are you like?

The Parable of the Ten Bridesmaids

"Then the kingdom of heaven will be comparable to ten virgins, who took their lamps and went out to meet the bridegroom. Five of them were foolish, and five were prudent. For when the foolish took their lamps, they took no oil with them, but the prudent took oil in flasks along with their lamps. Now while the bridegroom was delaying, they all got drowsy and began to sleep. But at midnight there was a shout, 'Behold, the bridegroom! Come out to meet him.' Then all those virgins rose and trimmed their lamps. The foolish said to the prudent, 'Give us some of your oil, for our lamps are going out.' But the prudent answered, 'No, there will not be enough for us and you too; go instead to the dealers and buy some for yourselves.' And while they were going away to make the purchase, the bridegroom came, and those who were ready went in with him to the wedding feast; and the door was shut. Later the other virgins also came, saying, 'Lord, lord, open up for us.' But he answered, 'Truly I say to you, I do not know you.' Be on the alert then, for you do not know the day nor the hour." (Matthew 25:1–13)

Obviously, Jesus employs a Jewish wedding analogy, in which the eagerly awaited bridegroom came to "snatch away" the bride for the wedding feast on the night before the wedding itself, to drive home His message. Again, the imagery in this parable is very simple. The bridegroom is Jesus Christ. The five wise virgins, or bridesmaids, represent genuine believers. The five foolish bridesmaids picture unbelievers.

SIMILARITIES BETWEEN THE FOOLISH AND WISE BRIDESMAIDS	
Five Foolish Bridesmaids	Five Wise Bridesmaids
All Are Bridesmaids	All Are Bridesmaids
All Have Lamps	All Have Lamps
All Go out to Meet the Bridegroom	All Go out to Meet the Bridegroom
All Get Drowsy and Fall Asleep	All Get Drowsy and Fall Asleep

To all appearances, the two groups of bridesmaids all look exactly alike, but there's one key difference. The five wise virgins took enough oil with them while the five foolish virgins did not. One group was prepared, the other was not.

Some insist that the oil here is a symbol of the Holy Spirit. While that's possible, it's not necessary with parables to press every detail for some hidden meaning. Clearly, the main point Jesus drives home is that the wise bridesmaids were prepared while the foolish ones were not.

Life Lessons from the Parable of the Ten Virgins

1. Christ, the heavenly Bridegroom, may delay His coming longer than we think.
2. Christ's coming will catch most people totally by surprise. Stay awake!
3. Those who only profess Christ but do not actually possess Him can look a lot like true believers.
4. Only those who are truly prepared through saving faith in Christ will be ready when He comes.
5. When He does finally come there will be no delay. Time will have run out (25:10).

6. When He comes there will be no second chances. Those who aren't ready will be excluded from the heavenly wedding feast (25:11–12).

The Parable of the Talents

"For it is just like a man about to go on a journey, who called his own slaves and entrusted his possessions to them. To one he gave five talents, to another, two, and to another, one, each according to his own ability; and he went on his journey. Immediately the one who had received the five talents went and traded with them, and gained five more talents. In the same manner the one who had received the two talents gained two more. But he who received the one talent went away, and dug a hole in the ground and hid his master's money. Now after a long time the master of those slaves came and settled accounts with them. The one who had received the five talents came up and brought five more talents, saying, 'Master, you entrusted five talents to me. See, I have gained five more talents.' His master said to him,

'Well done, good and faithful slave. You were faithful with a few things, I will put you in charge of many things; enter into the joy of your master.' Also the one who had received the two talents came up and said, 'Master, you entrusted two talents to me. See, I have gained two more talents.' His master said to him, 'Well done, good and faithful slave. You were faithful with a few things, I will put you in charge of many things; enter into the joy of your master.' And the one also who had received the one talent came up and said, 'Master, I knew you to be a hard man, reaping where you did not sow and gathering where you scattered no seed. And I was afraid, and went away and hid your talent in the ground. See, you have what is yours.' But his master answered and said to him, 'You wicked, lazy slave, you knew that I reap where I did not sow and gather where I scattered no seed. Then you ought to have put my money in the bank, and on my arrival I would have received my money back with interest. Therefore take away the talent from him, and give it to the one who has the ten talents.' For to everyone who has, more shall be given, and he will have an abundance; but from the one who does not have, even what he does have shall be taken away. Throw out the worthless slave into the outer darkness; in that place there will be weeping and gnashing of teeth." (Matthew 25:14–30)

The imagery in this parable is obvious. The man going on the long journey represents Christ. The long period of time He is gone away pictures the interadvent age, or the time between Christ's ascension to heaven and His return. The talents represent the diverse blessings, opportunities, resources, natural abilities, spiritual gifts, positions, privileges, and responsibilities the Master gives to us as stewards or managers to oversee and administer on His behalf. The time of settling accounts, when the slaves appear before the Master, illustrates the final day of reckoning when all must appear before the Lord.

The five-talent and two-talent slaves represent true believers whose ultimate desire is to serve and invest for the Master. The one talent slave depicts an unbeliever whose stewardship was totally unfaithful.

Life Lessons from the Parable of the Talents

1. A key to successful serving is to recognize that all we have is from God. (vv. 20, 22).

2. Christ predicted He would be gone for a "long time" (v. 19). It's now been almost two thousand years.

3. The greater the faithfulness in this life, the greater the reward and responsibility in the next (vv. 21, 23).

4. Rewards for investing your talents are huge. Five talents and two talents brought charge over "many things" (vv. 21, 23). A little bit invested wisely for the Master in this life will bring great reward.

5. Your talents are your test. What you do with your talents ultimately reveals what you really think about the Savior. The third slave didn't invest the talent. Why? He said he did it because the Master was harsh and exacting (vv. 24–25). But if that were really true he would have at least put it in the bank. No, this slave didn't invest because he was "lazy" (v. 26). He didn't want to bother. He made pretense of commitment, but in reality he refused to serve the Lord. He was too involved in his own interests—in serving himself. The first two involved their whole lives in investing the talent. What they thought of

the Master was revealed in what they did with the talents. Indeed, your talents are your test.

6. A day of final accounting before the Master is coming for every person, when our stewardship will be called to account (v. 19).

7. Hell is a terrible place of utter loss, darkness, despair and conscious torment (vv. 28–30).

Which servant are you? Do you have a personal relationship with the Master?

"What Then?"

William Gladstone was one of Great Britain's foremost leaders during the nineteenth century. Not only was he a brilliant statesman, he was also a devout Christian. One day, a young man came to see him to talk about his future. As the two sat across the desk from each other, Gladstone asked the young man what he proposed to do.

He was interested in going to Cambridge or Oxford University to pursue a good education.

Gladstone said, "That's good. A man needs a good foundation and I think that is wise. What then?"

"Well, sir, I thought that when I graduate from college I could get a job in one of the law firms and gain some practical experience because there are many things that I'll learn there that I'll never learn in school"

"That's wise, that's very wise. What then?"

"What I'd really like to do is serve in the government, and if I do well in law, perhaps one day I can stand first seat in Commons and be involved in the governing of the world through the government of Great Britain."

Gladstone said, "I appreciate that. We need men in government who are here because they are dedicated to a course. That's splendid. What then?"

"Well, sir, I thought if I did well with my party that perhaps sometime along the way they might choose me to be prime minister—to sit where you sit and to make an impact that way."

"Well, somebody has to sit here. That's good that you're going to aim that high. What then?"

"Well, sir, I have been keeping a diary, and I suspect that if I'm able to do these things, I could write my memoirs and pass on to other folks like myself the lessons that I've learned along the way."

"That's good. That can be a real help to folks. I think that's wise. What then?"

"Well, sir…like any man, I guess it would be time for me to die."

"Yes, whether all your goals are achieved, no matter where you sit, ultimately we are reduced there. What then?"

"Well…I have been so busy making my plans that I haven't had much time for religion. I do plan to get around to it, but I hadn't really thought about that. That's, you know, just not been in my thinking."

William Gladstone stood up and said, "Young man, you'd better get right home. Get down by the side of your bed, open up your Bible, and think life through to its very end."

As we look ahead to earth's final days, to our own final days, we need to ask that question—"What then?"

If you have never come to Jesus to receive Him as your personal Savior from sin, why not do so right now? Simply accept Him by taking freely of what He's done for you. While there are no magic words that bring salvation, a simple prayer like this can be used to express your faith in Jesus Christ.

Lord, thank You for taking my place on the cross.
I come now and take freely of
Your salvation from sin.
I accept You and all that You did for me.
Thank You for saving my soul. Amen.

May all who read these pages be ready to meet the heavenly Bridegroom when He comes.

The Master *is* coming!

May we live faithfully for Him until that day.

"Be on the alert then, for you do not know the day nor the hour" (Matthew 25:13).

The publisher and author would love to hear your
comments about this book.
Please contact us at:
www.multnomah.net/signsofthetimes

NOTES

1. The basic idea for this section was adapted from David Jeremiah, *Jesus' Final Warning* (Nashville: Word Publishing, 1999), 7–20.
2. Ibid., 9.
3. Charles Caldwell Ryrie, *The Best Is Yet to Come* (Chicago: Moody Press, 1981), 7–8.
4. There is a fourth view that some hold that we can call "The Double Fulfillment View." Adherents to this view argue that the Olivet Discourse was fulfilled in A.D. 70, but that the events of the destruction of Jerusalem point beyond historical fulfillment to the Great Tribulation that will be faced by God's people during the reign of Antichrist. See Kim Riddlebarger, *A Case for Amillennialism: Understanding the End Times* (Grand Rapids, Mich.: Baker Book House, 2003), 160–79. While this understanding of the events in Matthew 24 is possible, I reject the whole notion of double fulfillment of prophecies as an unacceptable method of interpretation.
5. John F. Walvoord, *Matthew: Thy Kingdom Come* (Chicago: Moody Press, 1974), 193.

6. For a thorough examination, critique, and rebuttal of the preterist view, see Tim LaHaye and Thomas Ice, gen. eds., *The End Times Controversy: The Second Coming Under Attack* (Eugene, Ore.: Harvest House Publishers, 2003).

7. Walvoord, *Matthew*, 182–4.

8. In the Old Testament, the fig tree was often used as a symbol for the nation of Israel, so many Bible interpreters understand this parable in that light. But I believe that Jesus is simply using a natural illustration that anyone can understand. He is saying that just as one can tell that summer is near by the blossoming of the fig tree, so those alive during the Tribulation will be able to see that His coming is near when the signs He has just listed (in Matthew 24:4–31) begin to happen. See Mark Hitchcock, *What on Earth Is Going On?* (Sisters, Ore.: Multnomah Publishers, 2002), 41–2.

9. The seven-year length of the future Tribulation is based on Daniel 9:27.

10. John F. MacArthur, *The Second Coming* (Wheaton, Ill.: Crossway Books, 1999), 81.

11. Geoffrey Cowley, "How Progress Makes Us Sick," *Newsweek* (May 5, 2003), 34.

12. These activities are described in detail in the apocryphal book of First Maccabees 1:4–59

13. Arnold Fruchtenbaum, *The Footsteps of the Messiah* (Tustin, Calif.: Ariel Ministries, 1983), 174.

14. Daniel 12:11 says that the abomination of desolation will stand in the holy place for 1,290 days. That's the final three-and-a-half years of the Tribulation (1,260 days) plus thirty extra days. Why an extra thirty days? When Jesus returns at his Second Coming at the end of the Tribulation, Antichrist

will be destroyed, but evidently the image will remain in the temple for another thirty days beyond that time, and then it, too, will be removed and destroyed.

15. Randall Price, *The Coming Last Days Temple* (Eugene, Ore.: Harvest House Publishers, 1999), 592.

16. J. C. Ryle, *Matthew, the Crossway Classic Commentaries*, ed. Alister McGrath and J. I. Packer (Wheaton, Ill.: Crossway Books, 1993), 232.

17. Several of these points were taken from John F. MacArthur, Jr., *The Second Coming of the Lord Jesus Christ*, Study Notes (Panorama City, Calif.: Word of Grace Communications, 1981), 1.

18. Walvoord, *Matthew*, 193–4.

END TIMES ANSWERS

WHAT ON EARTH IS GOING ON?
Pierce through the post-9/11 clouds of sensationalism and skepticism with prophecy expert Mark Hitchcock as he gives a balanced view of today's major global developments signaling Christ's return.
ISBN 1-57673-853-1

IS AMERICA IN BIBLE PROPHECY?
Will America suffer a great fall? Find out what's in store for the world's superpower in the coming days with prophecy scholar and pastor Mark Hitchcock.
ISBN 1-57673-496-X

THE COMING ISLAMIC INVASION OF ISRAEL
Mark Hitchcock shows how events today may be setting the stage for the fulfillment of Ezekiel's prediction—a Russian-Islamic confederation of nations will invade Israel and be destroyed by God.
ISBN 1-59052-048-3

IS THE ANTICHRIST ALIVE TODAY?
Is the Antichrist alive today, right now, in this generation? Prophecy expert Mark Hitchcock discusses five current events preparing the world for the Antichrist's reign.
ISBN 1-59052-075-0

SEVEN SIGNS OF THE END TIMES
Are you noticing the symptoms of the end of the world? Get an expert opinion. Discover seven specific signs the Bible says to look for.
ISBN 1-59052-129-3

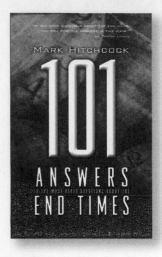

101 ANSWERS TO THE MOST ASKED QUESTIONS ABOUT THE END TIMES

The end is near! Or is it? The Antichrist is alive and well today! *Or is he?* The church is about to be raptured and will certainly escape the Tribulation…*right?* When it comes to the end times, there's so much confusion. Preachers with elaborate charts share their theories about Revelation and other prophetic books of the Bible. "Ah, Babylon stands for the United States," they say. But then other teachers share their theories: "No, Babylon stands for the Roman Catholic Church, or the European Union, or the literal Babylon rebuilt in Iraq…." *Would somebody please shoot straight with me?* Finally, someone has. Gifted scholar and pastor Mark Hitchcock walks you gently through Bible prophecy in an engaging, user-friendly style. Hitchcock's careful examination of the topic will leave you feeling informed and balanced in your understanding of events to come…in our time.

ISBN 1-57673-952-X

THE SECOND COMING OF BABYLON

Stirrings in Iraq—is Babylon back? The Bible says that Babylon will be rebuilt and become the economic center of the world. Even now the ruins of the ancient city—just sixty miles south of Baghdad, Iraq—are quietly stirring. What does it mean for America? For Israel? For every person alive today? Are we living in the last days of earth as we know it? Find out, from Bible prophecy expert Mark Hitchcock…

- How the focus of the world will shift back to Babylon
- How Antichrist will make Babylon his capital
- How the kingdoms of earth will fade as Babylon rises
- The false powers of Antichrist will grow
- How prophecy will be fulfilled—and Babylon finally destroyed!

ISBN 1-59052-251-6

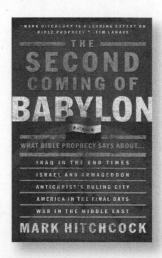